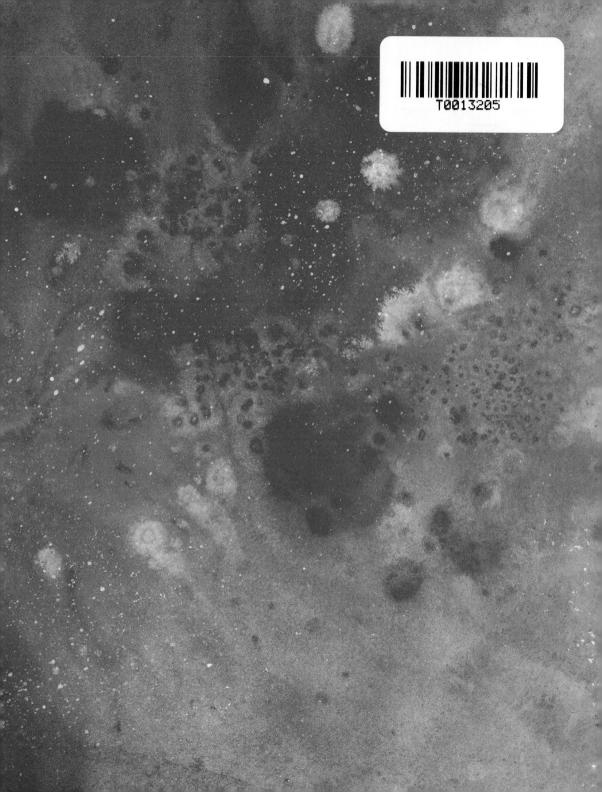

a magical night journey

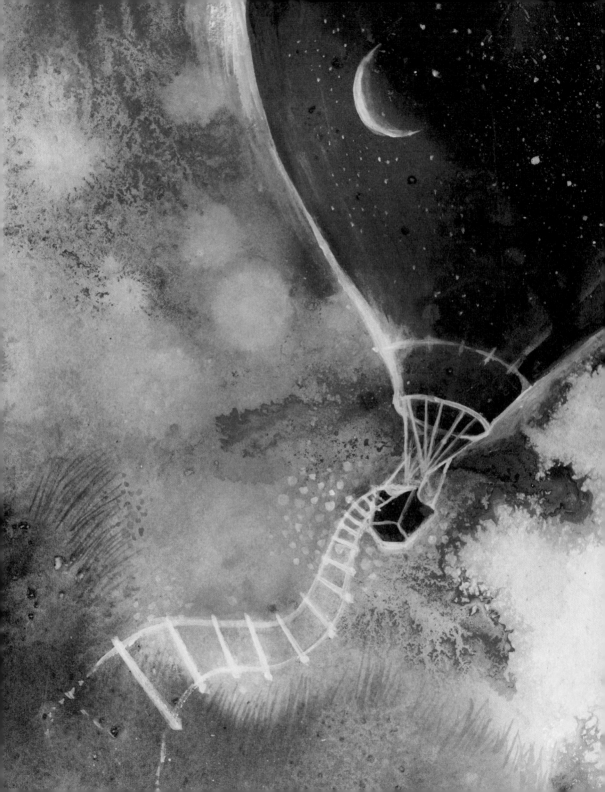

a magical night journey

FINDING WONDER AND SERENITY UNDER THE MOON AND STARS

AMY T. WON

CICO BOOKS
LONDON NEW YORK

Published in 2022 by CICO Books
An imprint of Ryland Peters & Small Ltd
20–21 Jockey's Fields   341 E 116th St
London WC1R 4BW   New York, NY 10029

www.rylandpeters.com

10 9 8 7 6 5 4 3 2 1

A CIP catalog record for this book is available from
the Library of Congress and the British Library.

ISBN: 978-1-78249-925-1

Printed in China

Commissioning editor: Kristine Pidkameny
Senior commissioning editor: Carmel Edmonds
Senior designer: Emily Breen
Art director: Sally Powell
Head of production: Patricia Harrington
Publishing manager: Penny Craig
Creative director: Leslie Harrington
Publisher: Cindy Richards

MIX
Paper from
responsible sources
FSC
www.fsc.org   FSC® C008047

contents

wonder-walking is a simple
practice of wandering with our
senses and imagination, and
is all we need to explore
everyday enchantment.

introduction

Imagine a world of magic right under your nose—one you've known but haven't really understood. Imagine feeling like explorers of times past, stepping into a world that is at once wondrous yet mysterious, terrifying yet fascinating.

We live in a time when so much is understood, has been documented, and has been explored, examined, and placed on a virtual platter for us to discover. It seems as if, short of participating in an expensive deep sea expedition, or shrinking oneself down to fit into current space rovers, there are no more frontiers left for the individual to discover. How lucky our ancestors were, to step into a nearby wood and find treasures untold and mysteries to unravel!

However, there is yet a hidden world most of us have not fully explored—one we think we know, but have often overlooked; one we need not travel very far to uncover. In fact, we can begin exploring it this very night.

The night offers a journey few of us have embarked on purposefully. We know of it; we might occasionally celebrate the moon and the stars, and we recognize when light shifts to dark at the end of the day. But all too often, the night is an afterthought—a lamentation of the day ending with tasks yet to be finished, of having to put away books, work, and toys. But the night, oh, the night is full of hidden magic. And the wonder-walk—a simple practice of wandering with our senses and imagination—is all we need to explore this last frontier of everyday enchantment.

This book is about our evolving relationship with the bewitching, sunless hours between dusk and dawn—which I like to call the nocturne—but also a journey of discovering wonder and serenity when we take that simple walk under the glorious night sky.

I hope you'll delight in traversing the wild dark with me through these illustrated pages, and that doing so inspires you to examine your own relationship with the nocturne and to learn, as I have, to be relaxed and even enjoy the hidden, the unknown, and the unseen. To help you along this night journey, I've scattered, like Hansel's breadcrumbs, a trail of journal and observation prompts throughout, as well as suggestions for illuminating nighttime activities you can undertake on your own or with fellow explorers, both indoors and outdoors under the moon and stars.

nocturne: "a romantic or dreamy picture of a night scene in art or music."

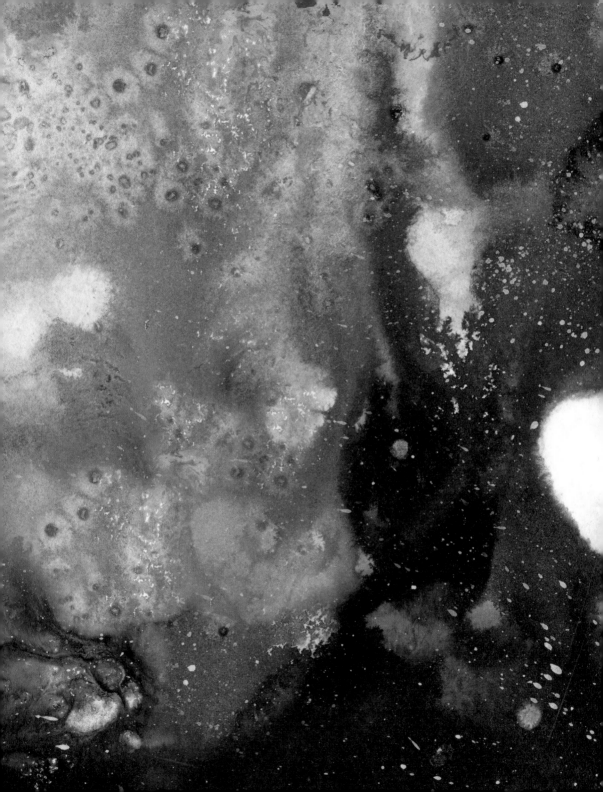

into the dark

What will we discover when we set forth into the darkness with intention? What wonders lie hidden in the shadows, in the unexplored places of our everyday lives, in our minds and hearts?

night walking

I have a confession: I am afraid of the dark. For a very long time, I slept with the lights on in new places, I was afraid to walk at night by myself in shadowy areas, and I never ventured into a forest after sundown. There was an encyclopedia book about the ocean I loved as a child but I was terrified of the chapter on creatures of the abyss—a place of permanent night where the sun never penetrates—and skipped quickly over these pages with my gaze averted whenever I reread the book.

I don't remember where this fear originated but I suspect it's because of my very vivid imagination. Since then I've learned to love the absence of light, especially outdoors under an expansive indigo sky. I've grown less wary of strolling through the woods at twilight, and have even gone camping in the wilderness by myself, though I may have taken along a tiny battery-powered nightlight. And I've discovered that what we don't know scares us, and that I share my fears with all my ancestors who have walked in the night before me. Our enjoyment, feelings, and thoughts of these dark hours outdoors have long been shaped by disorientation and unfamiliarity with lightlessness.

In many ways, the night journey is about readjusting our relationship with both discomfort and the unknown, so that we can actually see the untold wonders hiding in the night.

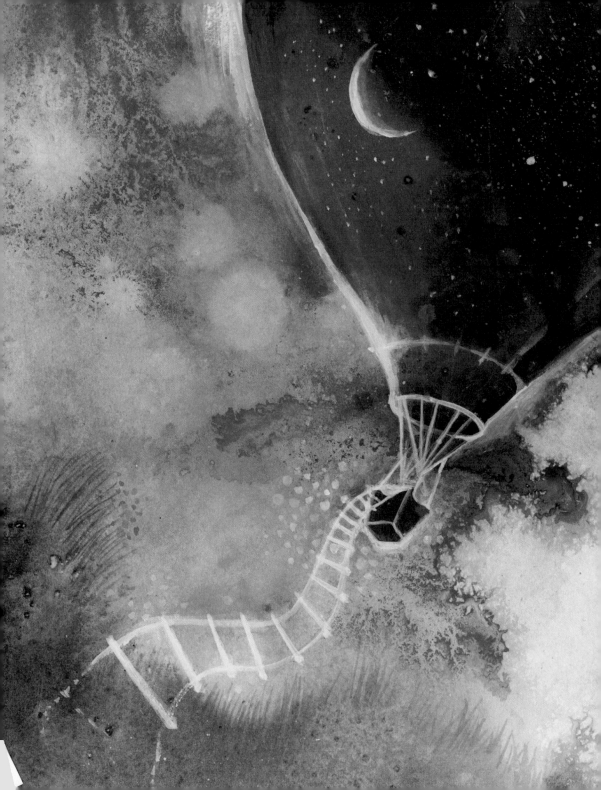

In my journey of reconnecting with the nocturne, I stumbled upon some of the most enchanting and mysterious aspects of our lives on Earth—the faraway, celestial worlds we will never know, the animals and plants we've heard of but never seen, and natural phenomena as astonishing as any magical spell in fairy tales. Beyond that, the nocturne holds many hidden archetypal meanings of our soul journey: confronting our shadows and fears, being comfortable with uncertainty, and navigating what we cannot see.

Over the next few pages, you'll find some creative and contemplative activities to help you prepare to explore the nocturnal world.

an adventure of wonder awaits you.

create a night journal

Have you always been fascinated by the night but not been sure why? Creating a night journal is a great way to explore this in greater depth, and if you're a creative spirit, it may even become a source of inspiration for writings, paintings, or sculptures.

You've probably heard about dream journals and morning journals. A night journal is a close cousin, except that it captures everything that you feel, think, and experience about the magical time between dusk and dawn when you're awake and aware.

I recommend using a blank book in a portable size that you can not only write in, but also paint, sketch, and collage in, if you'd like to. You can start with a simple black journal (try splattering white paint on the cover to create a night sky), a beautiful leather journal embossed with the moon and stars on the cover, or a lovingly hand-bound one with a mix of white and indigo pages.

If you're not ready to dedicate an entire blank notebook to the night, you can begin with the journal pages in this book and see where they take you.

go ahead and be creative, the night is your oyster!

SUGGESTED SECTIONS FOR YOUR JOURNAL

You could journal in long-form ramblings, but you may prefer to organize them into neat little sections. Here are some suggestions for how you might divide your journal:

✦ Memories

✦ Feelings and thoughts

✦ Flora and fauna sightings

✦ Soul and symbolism

We'll also be discussing some of these sections later in this book, so do look out for them. What other sections can you think of?

Alternatively, you could create a section for each chapter of this book so that your journaling can follow along with your guided adventures.

a nocturnal meditation

Night time evokes different emotions in all of us. Whether it's a fear of the dark, a fascination for celestial worlds, or the only slice of sacred alone time you'll get in 24 hours, the journal exercises here will allow you to see what emerges from the shadows. You can capture your thoughts in the journal space provided or in your night journal (see pages 16–17).

Before you begin exploring the nocturne, take some time to set some intentions and contemplate the journey before you.

✦ What do you hope to discover about the night?

✦ What fascinates you about the night?

✦ Is there anything about the night that makes you uncomfortable?

Now find a quiet place to be with the night, whether on a walk after dusk, or while sitting by a window with a glimpse of the starry sky.

Ponder what these words mean to you:

✦ Nightfall ✦ Night ✦ Shadow

✦ Nocturne ✦ Darkness ✦ Dusk

_____

_____

_____

_____

_____

_____

_____

If you're a painter rather than a writer, you could create paintings or drawings of the night to express your feelings about the word prompts. You could also try poetry, photography, or collage—whichever medium works best for you.

create a night journey ritual

Having a night journey ritual means making sacred time for exploring the nocturne, whether you do it physically on a wonder-walk outdoors, while sitting by the window within view of the moon and stars, or through a creative or study project. Here are some suggestions.

A TWILIGHT OR NOCTURNAL WALK

Step outside for a few minutes by yourself or with loved ones after dark to enjoy the serenity of the night and explore wonders that are hidden in daylight. This could be in your neighborhood or simply your backyard.

A CREATIVE PROJECT

Work on a project inspired by the night: knit a sweater with the constellations, embroider the night sky in a wooden hoop, paint an owl lit by the moon, or write an ode to the coyote howling at midnight. As you explore the night, express how you feel creatively in your favorite artistic medium.

A NIGHT MEDITATION

Find a quiet spot at night where you can perform a sitting or walking meditation, whether outside, on a balcony, or even inside by the window. Immerse yourself in the sounds and sights of the night and let it help you cultivate serenity, mindfulness, and gratitude for the gifts of the nocturne.

ENJOY A NOCTURNAL STORY

Read a book, watch a movie, or listen to music inspired by the night. Study how others have explored and interpreted their nocturnal journeys to ignite your own adventures.

A NIGHT JOURNAL SESSION

Whichever night journey ritual you choose, record your thoughts, feelings, and discoveries in your night journal (see pages 16–17) to help you process and navigate your relationship with the nocturne.

MAKING IT INTO A RITUAL

Consider how often you'll spend time exploring the night. Is it something you'll do every evening? On weekends, or two or three times a week? Whatever you decide, try to remain consistent.

As you explore the night with this book, your favorite night adventures will come into the light. Together with the suggestions above, you should be able to create a journey ritual that awakens wonder and serenity every nightfall.

what will your night journey ritual involve?

nocturnal mood painting

One of my favorite forms of visual meditation involves pondering a mood painting like the one opposite.

Study the painting in a relaxed manner, with your eyes slightly soft-focus, and see if any scenes, feelings, or ideas emerge from the textures and colors. With a white or light-colored pen or pencil, draw what you see over the mood painting.

You can also note below the feelings, emotions, and thoughts that came up for you around this scene, with these questions to guide you:

✦ What do you see?

✦ What is emerging from the darkness?

✦ What do you think it means?

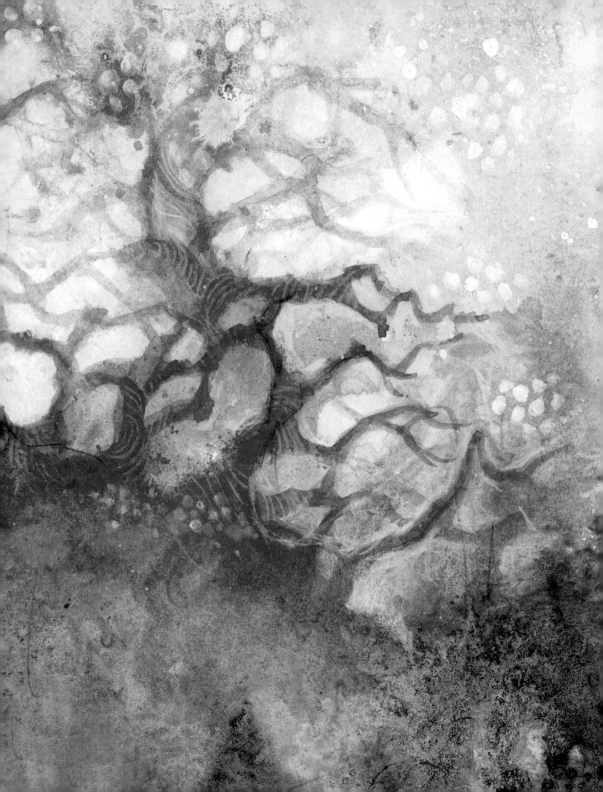

memories of the night

Our relationship with nighttime is years in the making. How we engage with it and what we think, love, and fear about it have been shaped through time. What long-forgotten treasures of the nocturne will we rediscover when we walk into our memories of the night?

early night memories

I lived in many houses growing up, but the one I remember the most sat on top of a hill, with a grand view of the valley below. I don't recall much of what the inside looked like, nor do I have many memories of life within it, but I have a very clear recollection of the hours spent outdoors under the night sky. I remember the glittering lights from the houses in the valley below us, all the deep conversations had with friends, and the laughter and merrymaking of the outdoor parties my parents threw under the canopy of stars.

memory-walking

One of the best ways to examine our relationship with the night is to re-experience our memories of it through an activity called "memory-walking" that I learned from artist and author Hannah Hinchman. To memory-walk, all you have to do is select a memory, close your eyes, and imagine yourself back in time, walking around the scene. Write down what you see. You'll probably find yourself recalling details that you thought you'd forgotten.

MEMORY-WALKING THE NIGHT

Try choosing a memory from childhood that took place outdoors after sundown, such as a birthday party, a festival or celebration with fireworks, or a camping trip. Begin your memory walk and write down what you see here or in your night journal (see pages 16–17).

TAKING IT FURTHER

When you've completed one or two memory-walks, you could explore your childhood experiences and how they've affected your current relationship with the night using the prompts below.

✦ What were you astonished by or afraid of in the absence of light as a child?

✦ How have you been shaped by your experiences of the dark outdoors?

✦ Did you learn to seek solace in the night from a young age?

✦ Did your friendship with the moon begin in your teen years or was there a significant event that brought the moon into your orbit?

✦ What was your first nocturnal memory?

night festivities

Night transforms places in ways we don't often think about. In the equatorial tropics where I grew up, daytime heat and humidity prohibited outdoor activities, and so nightfall was when the world truly came alive. This meant that throughout my younger years, the pleasant coolness in the dark hours after sunset was a special time for gathering and festivities.

It's not hard to see why, of all my memories of a tropical childhood, my favorites are ones from evening celebrations, like the magical Mid-Autumn Lantern Festival. During this special night, children carried delicate animal-shaped lanterns, made from wire and cellophane, around the neighborhood under the light of the full moon. It was one of the rare occasions that we children were allowed to be out by ourselves at night, and my recollections of it are filled with dreamy, joyous scenes of gathering and giggling around ethereal lights with friends, eating mooncakes, and remembering to walk ever so carefully so as not to put out the single candle that lit the lanterns from within.

a cherished nocturnal memory

Now that you have done a little bit of memory-walking, let's dig a little deeper into some of your favorite nighttime experiences in childhood, like mine of the lantern walk on the previous page.

While I still enjoy eating mooncakes during the Mid-Autumn Festival, I had long forgotten this magical little ritual in the dark outdoors that I looked forward to so much as a child, and so it's been wonderful to revisit these joyous times.

What is your most cherished memory of the night from childhood? For example, did you ever enjoy chasing fireflies in the evenings with your siblings or friends? Or do you have a fond memory of watching fireworks over the ocean? Memory-walk long-ago nights such as these, and try to visualize the role the nocturne played in making this such an enchanting time in your life.

details from your memory-walk of your cherished nocturnal experience

_____

_____

_____

_____

_____

_____

_____

_____

_____

_____

ways this event shaped who you are now

_____

_____

_____

_____

_____

_____

_____

_____

_____

_____

overcoming fear

By now, you've probably realized that how we respond to the night is both instinctive and learned. While our memories of the night shape the expectations we have of nightfall, they also reveal how much we're wary of it.

The places that are safe and familiar to us in the light of day can seem much less so in the dark. And because we're predominantly visual creatures with diminished eyesight in low light, it's natural to feel disoriented, threatened, and uncomfortable in the dark. Our senses are heightened to compensate for poor vision and what's unfamiliar feels strange and potentially dangerous.

It's important to be aware of these feelings of discomfort, because it helps us understand where they come from. This then enriches our relationship with the nocturne and allows us to experience it in deeper ways.

For me, growing up in the pre-digital age in a tiny town with no malls or cinemas meant that entertainment often consisted of simple outdoor activities. One of the highlights of my teenage years was an annual Scouts camping trip deep in the jungle, where it poured with rain every night we were there, every single year, without fail. We dug deep ditches around our oilskin and bamboo tents, scooped out water and leeches to stay comfortable, and played tag in the dark among the trees. Walking in the jungle after dusk requires special skill—no leaning against trees or sitting on the ground sight unseen, because there are too many lurking creatures about, such as giant fire ants, venomous snakes, poisonous caterpillars, and many others one would not like to encounter in the dark.

Nevertheless, these are by far my favorite memories of being outdoors at night growing up. It banded my fellow Scouts and me together—this exciting but strange sort of forced intimacy built camaraderie as we struggled to keep our sleeping areas dry, our uniforms clean, and our dignity intact.

In retrospect, these jungle nights helped me develop a tolerance for nocturnal discomfort that extended beyond my school years, preparing me for the kind of outdoor adventures I would seek out as an adult.

your memories of feeling uncomfortable being outdoors at night

_____

_____

_____

_____

_____

_____

_____

_____

_____

_____

transformation

Nightfall transforms an environment (and our perception of it) in ways we often take for granted. There are altered temperatures and humidity and changes in sounds, sights, and smells from the plants and animals that come alive after dusk. Our eyesight is less acute and reliable, and our other senses become heightened because we pay attention to environmental cues that are less significant in the bright light of day.

When I met my husband, he showed me a side of the nocturnal outdoors I hadn't known before. We went camping in the wilds of the southeastern United States, and I was delighted to find that in winter there are no bugs and I could lie down on the forest floor to admire the starry sky. He taught me how to build the best campfires and how to pay attention to moonrises. With him as my nocturnal guide in a new land, I've learned to listen out for owls conversing in hoots, to recognize the howls of coyotes in the distance, and to watch out for raccoon eyes in the dark while camping.

We've had some wondrous nocturnal adventures together, exploring my favorite places in darkness, an activity I avoided on my own. Together we've traversed various terrains that are vastly different in the night than they are under the harsh sun of noon. A rocky desert park becomes an eerie extraterrestrial landscape by night. An ordinary wood transforms into an enchanted moonlit forest, all silvery branches and dark shadows.

which of your favorite places are transformed by nighttime?

examine your nocturnal sensescape

Take a walk outdoors at night somewhere that it's almost completely dark, where your sensescape is transformed. If you aren't able to step outside, memory-walk (see page 28) a time when you've felt uncomfortable in the dark.

Examine how you feel as you wander around. Observe your five senses at work and if they are altered as night falls by pondering these questions:

✦ What do you see? Or not see? How does your impaired vision in the dark affect your experience of the night?

✦ What do you hear? Or not hear? How are the sounds different at night from during the day?

✦ What can you smell? Taste? How is it different from daytime?

✦ How does darkness affect your sense of touch? Are you more or less likely to reach for objects in your surroundings? Why?

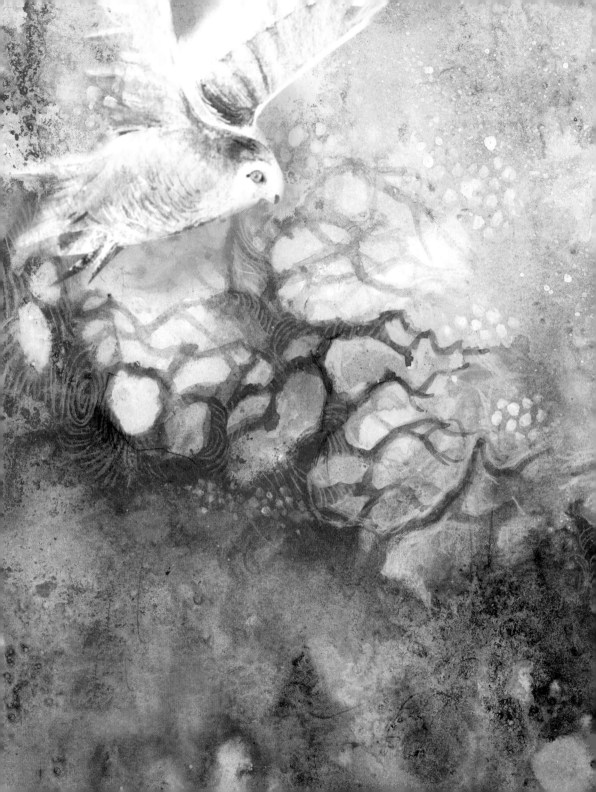

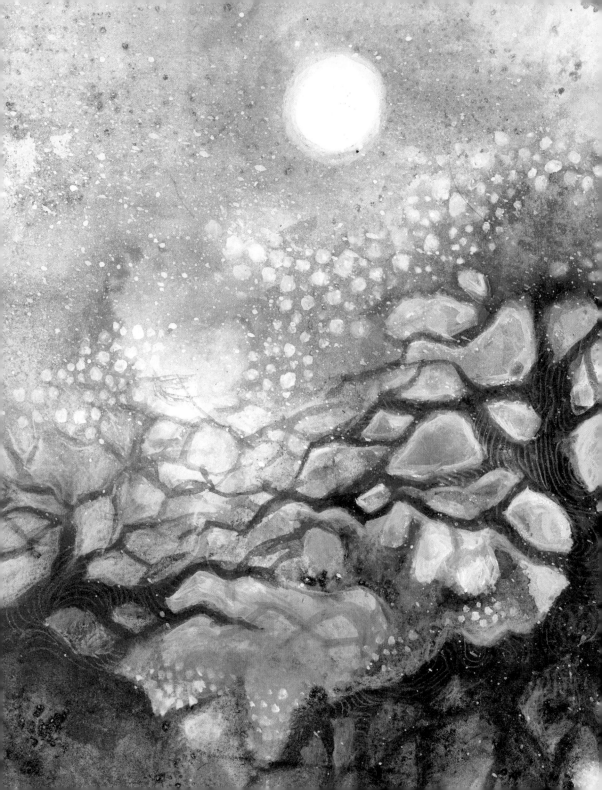

comparing night and day: a creative project

Identify a favorite place near where you live that you can safely access both day and night. Visit this place in the daytime and take a photograph, create a painting of it, or write about how it looks in bright light.

Then revisit this place at nightfall and repeat the process. You might have to use a tripod if you're photographing at night. A flashlight might also be necessary for drawing or writing in the dark.

If you're unable to travel far, try setting up a tripod in your backyard and create a time-lapse photograph of a plant, a tree, or a favorite view. Watch how this familiar place transforms when the sun sets and the moon and stars come up.

Compare your night and day creations. Observe how they evoke different feelings, thoughts, and moods. Why do you think this is? You can record your observations in your night journal (see pages 16–17) or in the space opposite.

observations of your day and night creations

_____

_____

_____

_____

_____

_____

_____

_____

_____

_____

_____

nocturnal companionship

The moon and I have been friends for a long time. In the stillness of the night when all the world is hushed, there is an illusion of solitude amid the shadows. Even so, I've never felt alone in the dark because the moon has been by my side throughout my journey in life, in every place I've lived in, on all my nocturnal walks—a quiet, steadfast companion for many years to come.

Why does the night feel more intimate and serene? What makes it so different from the bright light of day?

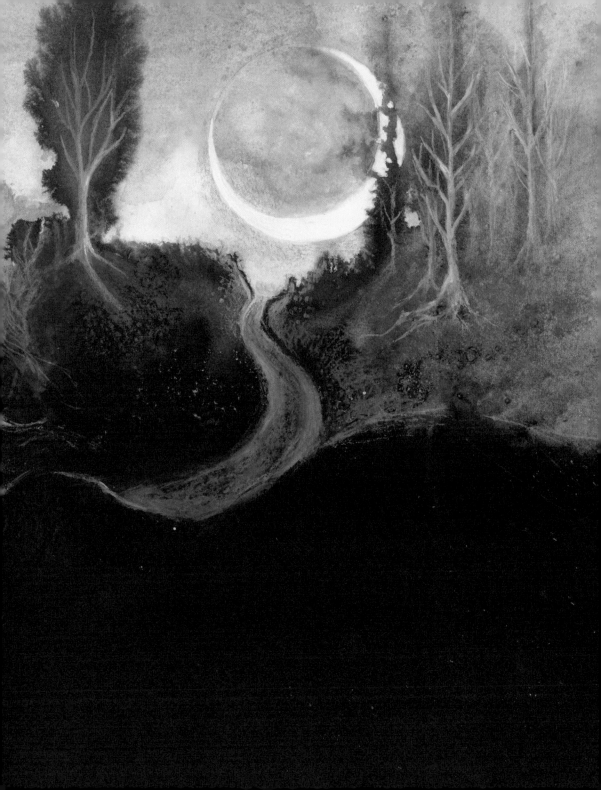

There is something about the nocturne that simultaneously unites and divides. Boundaries amplify at night with available light. Lit spaces of a home seen from outside a window reinforce spatial separation and underscore the contrast between inside and outside. In a gathering of friends around an outdoor firepit after dusk, the night is like an inky cloak of intimacy around a cozy milieu. It brings everyone closer together; hushed tones and dimmed eyesight unite them against the dark world beyond their circle of light. What we can't see does not exist, cannot distract.

It is this magical dance of visibility that makes our nocturnal walks far more intimate and serene than the same one by day. It's why we feel a kinship to the moon on our moonlit strolls. And it's why we remember a nocturnal conversation under the streetlamp far more than we do a similar one in daylight.

the intimacy of darkness

The next time you're outdoors at night, whether it's for an evening stroll or at an outdoor barbecue at a friend's place, pay attention to how you relate to familiar objects in the darkness of night.

✦ Do you feel closer to or more distant from the people, objects, and places around you?

✦ In what situations do you feel closer?

✦ In what situations do you feel more separate or apart?

✦ When does the night feel more serene? Why do you think this is?

things you've noticed about the night

your ideas, feelings, and thoughts about the night

_____

_____

_____

_____

_____

_____

_____

_____

_____

_____

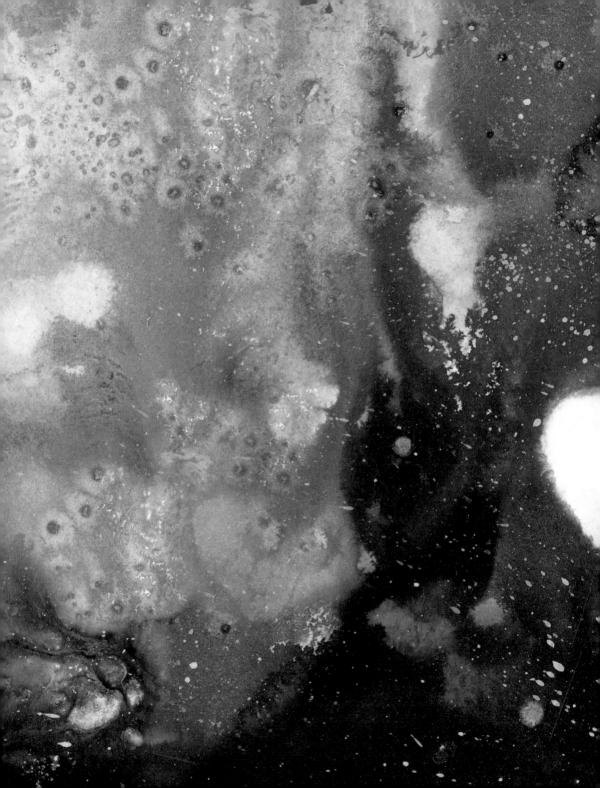

tales of twilight

We sometimes forget that we have lived
all our history with as many nights as
we did days, and that the night shapes
much of our understanding of the
world. When we travel through these
captivating tales of the nocturne, we
reconnect to what the night has always
meant to our human journey.

campfire stories

For early humans, the night was a time of rest, ceremony, and story. While daytime was for work and survival, night was reserved for spiritual, recreational, and emotional matters. With the setting of the sun, the brutality of a day spent hunting or foraging faded with the light and our ancestors gathered around a hearth or campfire to sing, dance, tell stories, and enact rituals against the backdrop of playful shadows, embracing the darkness.

While the focus remains theoretically the same in modern times, somewhere along the way, we went from active participants in a communal ritual to passive consumption of digital entertainment in isolation, with artificial lights all but guaranteeing that the night is a distant concept.

I'm often reminded of how much more alive I feel in the rare moments when I'm able to unplug and escape into the wilderness for a camping trip with family or friends. When there's nothing standing between me and the night, the connection is palpable, and I am almost painfully aware of my surroundings—the sound of crickets, the Milky Way above, and the warm glow of the campfire and companionship.

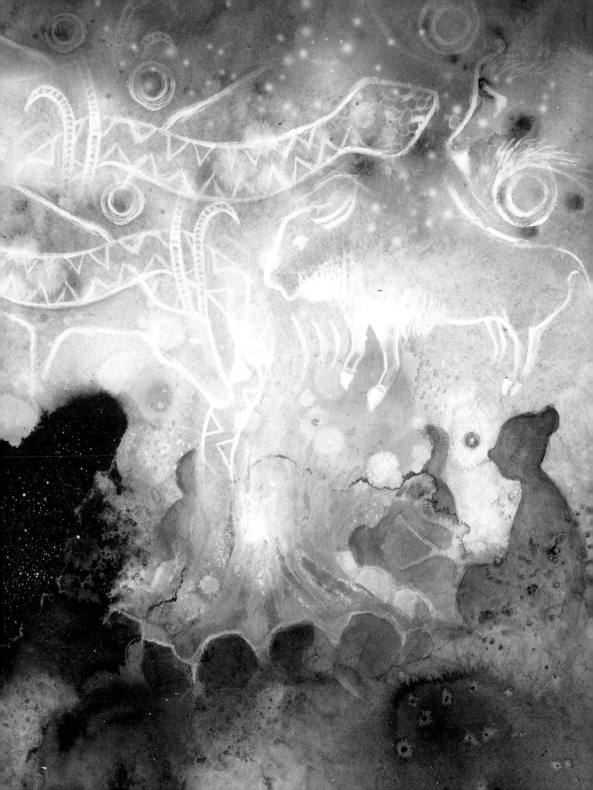

live like early humans

Recreate the convivial warmth of the night as our ancestors would have experienced. Explore how it changes the way you live the hours between dusk and dawn. While it might not always be possible to get away for a camping trip, see if you can recreate a hearth for you and your companion(s) to gather around. You could try an outdoor firepit, a chiminea, a mini barbecue, or even a plate of candles in your backyard or balcony. Turn off all artificial lights and phones, leave the portable speaker behind, and trade stories about your days or about what you see and hear around you. Regale each other with jokes and songs.

As you get more comfortable with this ancient way of experiencing the night, introduce feasting to this nocturnal adventure—a tray of snacks, skewers of barbecued food, or steaming buns. You could even cook a meal outdoors as you trade stories.

Here are a few other activities you might like to incorporate into your evening festivities:

✦ Create a shadow puppet theatre for young ones.

✦ Observe and point out constellations in the night sky (see also page 61).

✦ Listen out for hidden creatures.

✦ Learn how to build a fire and keep it kindled.

CREATING NIGHTTIME RITUALS

Reflect on how spending time outdoors in the evening contrasts with your regular nights in front of the television. Can these activities be the norm rather than twice-a-year special occasions? What do you enjoy the most, and what will you ritualize or incorporate into your life regularly?

_____

_____

_____

_____

_____

_____

_____

_____

_____

_____

keepers of the stars

Once upon a time, Pacific Islanders of Polynesia and Micronesia sailed thousands of miles across the Pacific Ocean against the wind, guided only by birds, waves, and the celestial stars.

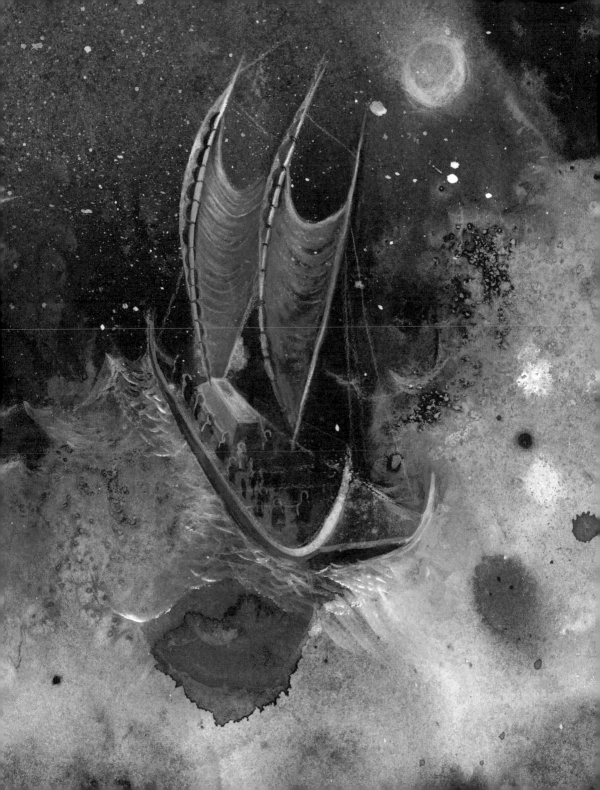

When I think about the greatest feats of human exploration throughout history, nothing is more fascinating to me than stories about the ancient nautical navigational techniques of these Islanders, still in use by some of them today. When we compare their methods to the complex instruments and systems of modern nautical navigation, it's mind-blowing what the Islanders were able to accomplish simply through careful attention to nature. By learning and memorizing where the stars rose and set in the expansive sky, known as the star compass, and by observing the waves and bird flight patterns, ancient Islanders were able to navigate across vast expanses of the ocean, over 2,000 miles each way.

Both their ability to navigate without instruments and the unrelenting level of attentiveness to their surroundings necessary for success are beyond our modern imagination. How often in our current life of GPS and map apps do we find ourselves relying on our powers of observation for wayfinding? Rarely, if ever.

celestial way-finding

Spend some time stargazing to see how well you can orientate yourself in the night with the help of nature's heavenly signposts.

Go for a night-time walk, taking a blanket if you can, and find a spot to lie down or sit and look at the stars above. Using a guidebook, such as Tristan Gooley's *The Lost Art of Reading Nature's Signs*, or a stargazing app, start by identifying the North Star or Polaris, which helps you tell where north is. There are a few ways to do this—locating two constellations, the Big Dipper and Cassiopeia, are helpful for pinpointing the North Star.

Get comfortable as you situate yourself in the night sky. As you study the vast celestial heavens above, ponder these questions:

✦ The Polynesian Islanders traveled across the ocean to explore and settle distant lands with the heavens as a guide. Imagine how wayfinding might have felt for the Islanders out in the open ocean in their double-hulled canoes.

✦ Where would you go if you could go anywhere right now? What would you be doing? What would you see?

✦ Using the celestial heavens as a symbol of uncharted territory and the North Star as your soul's destination, dream about the life you would like to navigate toward.

what you imagine the life of a wayfinder was like

_____

_____

_____

_____

_____

_____

_____

_____

_____

_____

description of your soul's destination and how you might get there

_____

_____

_____

_____

_____

_____

_____

_____

_____

constellation myths

One of my favorite experiences of the night sky took place indoors in a planetarium, with the voice of a celestial travel guide taking me on a journey through the starlit heavens. As she pointed out the constellations and recounted epic tales of immortal gods and goddesses, I watched in awe as magical lines connected the stars into pictures before my eyes. This is one of the stories she told:

One day, the archer-goddess Diana was challenged by her brother Apollo that she could not shoot a distant object in the water. Unbeknownst to Diana, it was her beloved Orion wading through the ocean. She let off a fatal shot and when the waves brought Orion's body to the shore, Diana cried many tears for her love and placed him among the stars.

Thousands of years ago, ancient humans took the vast and unimaginable tapestry of stars overhead and spun tales in such a way as to make it more relatable and less distant. It took considerably more imagination than I exercised, sitting in the comfort of a planetarium with a digital projector as an aid. These days, when I study the night sky on a nocturnal wonder-walk, tracing the constellations in my mind's eye, I am reminded of the inspiring magic of the night and our human capacity to imagine and make meaning of its secrets.

exploring stories of the stars

On a clear, moonless night, observe the starry night sky and ponder these questions:

✦ Why have the stars inspired such epic tales throughout human civilization?

✦ Why do you think those stories were told in the first place?

Study well-known myths about the constellations, such as those about Orion, Andromeda, Cassiopeia, Ursa Major, and Ursa Minor. Which tales do you find most fascinating? How do they help you see, remember, and navigate the night sky?

_____

_____

_____

_____

_____

_____

_____

the origin stories of night & day

I've always wondered what it would be like to live in the times before science, before we knew about the solar system and our place in the immeasurable universe. While there are clearly benefits to inhabiting a world we can predict and extrapolate from, we have also sacrificed much of its mystery and wonder in service of knowledge.

Some of the most beautiful and imaginative stories throughout human civilization have been origin stories of night and day. We can only wonder what our ancestors must have felt as they stood at the edge of the day, watching a large glowing ball of light sink into the horizon as darkness descended; what it was like to look up and notice a dusky roof of glittering pinpricks and the rising silvery lantern of the moon.

if we didn't know what we know now, how would we make sense of a world in which we live half our lives in the light and the other half in the dark?

While there's no way of erasing my modern understanding of the phenomenon of night, it's possible for me to temporarily suspend my knowledge by visiting its wondrous origin stories. One of my favorites is this Native American story of the Owl and the Rabbit:

"Night, night, night," said the owl.

"Light, light, light," said the rabbit.

And so they went on for a time.

Be careful what you say, the owl's friends warned him. Be careful what you say, the rabbit's friends warned him.

But it was too late. In the middle of the battle, the owl tripped on his tongue and said night, night, night, light. And that was how night and day were born.

explore origin stories

Imagine how you would understand night and day if you lived in an age before science. Explore this by reading origin stories of the night. There are various places you might find these stories:

✦ Indigenous stories of your homeland or ancestry

✦ Popular folklore or folktales of a country or region

✦ Religious texts like the Bible or the Quran

✦ Mythologies of the world, including Greek, Roman, Norse, Japanese, Hindu, and Aztec

Journal or ponder these questions:

✦ What is your favorite tale? Why?

✦ What did you learn about the experience and significance of night and day through this story?

CREATIVE PROJECT: WRITE YOUR OWN ORIGIN STORY

Go on a wonder-walk at dusk and watch the day change into night.
Imagine if you had no scientific knowledge of why this happens and
write your own origin story.

archetypes & symbols

Throughout history, the night has been connected with abundant analogies of the human experience, from the fear and darkness in the human psyche—death, the underworld, and the shadow self—to the enchanted and mystical worlds of shapeshifters, faerie folk, and the wise inner self. To embrace the night is to allow oneself to be transformed: the absence of light disrupts the senses and amplifies discomfort and uncertainty, compelling us to face our fears of what we cannot see and do not understand. In confronting the menacing, unpredictable otherness of the night, we relinquish its hold on us and allow the wonders of the nocturne to take its place.

finding truth in the dark

Turn off all artificial lights in your room or home and sit by the window in view of the night sky, if possible. Settle into the darkness and let any fear or discomfort wash over you. Be with your own thoughts as you turn your attention toward the absence of light, the nocturnal scene outdoors, and the stillness of the night.

Think of a fear or shadow of the nighttime that you might want to release into the dark.

✦ Are you afraid of the dark?

✦ Do the howls of coyotes make your skin crawl?

✦ What wonders would you notice in return if you let go of your distrust of the night?

If you're able to take a nocturnal wonder-walk outdoors, ponder these questions in the darkest parts of your stroll.

_____

_____

_____

_____

_____

CREATIVE PROJECT: EXPLORE SYMBOLS

Make a list of archetypes and symbols of the night that come to mind right now. Here are a few to get you started:

✦ Owls

✦ Bats

✦ Fireflies

✦ Vampires

✦ The moon

Which archetype of the night are you drawn to right now? What does it represent to you? Draw, paint, collage or write a poem about this.

fairy tales

I've realized that many of my favorite fairy tales from childhood have an element of the nocturne in them, which intensifies, for me, each story's feeling of enchantment and magic. In some of these stories, the night is a character itself, representing darkness, sorcery, mystery, fear, and uncertainty.

As fairy tales are the purest form of symbolic storytelling, its simplistic structure a mirror to the soul, exploring the role nighttime plays in our favorite tales can be a profound way to unearth what the nocturne truly means to us.

THE SHOES THAT WERE DANCED TO PIECES

The breathtaking image of twelve beautiful princesses decked out in ballroom finery, in twelve magical boats rowed by twelve handsome princes on a glassy lake under a moonlit sky, surrounded by glittering trees of silver and gold, never fails to enchant me, whether it's Kay Nielsen's glorious illustration or *Faerie Tale Theatre*, the old TV series on fairy tales (1982–87).

Dig a little deeper and this magical vignette belies a dark, nocturnal tale of deception, death, and a dreamlike underworld full of secrets. As the story goes, a king discovers that his twelve daughters' shoes are danced to pieces every morning, despite locking them in their room at night. He challenges princes of near and far to discover where they go when everyone is abed, with death as punishment for failure. But each time a prince is left with the princesses at night, he falls into a deep sleep and wakes up none the wiser.

Finally, a wounded soldier, aided by advice from an old woman and a magic invisibility cloak, finds himself on this quest. He rejects the princesses' offer of drugged wine and follows them unseen through a trapdoor under a bed, descending into a magical nocturnal underworld. He travels with them across the lake into a grand palace, and observes as the twelve princesses dance with the twelve princes all through the night until their shoes are ruined.

When he recounts his discovery to the king, he is rewarded with the oldest princess's hand and lives happily ever after. I find this tale immensely fascinating in its interweaving of the night with sleep, dreams, deception, and the underworld, and I'm often left with more questions than answers:

✦ Why is the door to this nocturnal world under a bed? What does this mean?

✦ Who are the princes and what does the nightly dancing mean?

✦ What is the significance of the nocturnal boat journey over the lake to the ball at the palace?

HANSEL AND GRETEL

This classic tale about a little boy and girl abandoned deep in the woods by their woodcutter father and stepmother has bewitched me for as long as I can remember. I recall many hours replaying it on a read-along cassette tape, tracing over the vivid illustrations in the accompanying picture book, holding my breath as the children journeyed with their parents into the dark woods, visualizing the moonlit path of pebbles Hansel left behind and feeling their growing trepidation when their parents did not reappear to fetch them. I could imagine their terror at being lost in the dark on the second night when they discovered their breadcrumb trail home had been eaten by birds.

It was the stuff childhood nightmares are made of, and nothing enthralled me more than to read about Hansel and Gretel's eventual triumph over the wicked witch at the gingerbread house, and then finding their way back home to their father.

The night in this fairy tale heightens the fear of being lost in a dark forest—of never finding one's way out again—but also offers a glimmer of hope as the moon shines on the trail of pebbles leading home. We understand their plight viscerally when we read of the children huddling together in the forest at night, shadows all around. And when they finally make their way out, we feel, as they do, like the sun is rising after a dark, fearful trek into the abyss, the joy all the more piercing for its contrast.

exploring the night in fairy tales

Reread the famous Brothers Grimm tales discussed on pages 78–81 in their original forms and ponder these questions:

✦ Which of these two fairy tales attracts you the most?

✦ What emotions come up for you during the night scenes?

_____

_____

_____

_____

_____

_____

_____

_____

deciphering symbols

These two fairy tales are filled with nocturnal symbols. What do you think the following symbols mean?

✦ The Shoes That Were Danced to Pieces: the trapdoor under the bed; the boat ride across the shimmering lake at night; the twelve princes and their palace ball

✦ Hansel and Gretel: the moonlit path of pebbles; the forest at night

creative project: fairy tale art

Can you think of other fairy tales and myths that are set in the night?
Create a piece of art in your favorite medium (such as drawing,
painting, collage, or writing) inspired by the most evocative nocturnal
scene from one of these stories.

_____

_____

_____

_____

_____

_____

_____

_____

_____

_____

_____

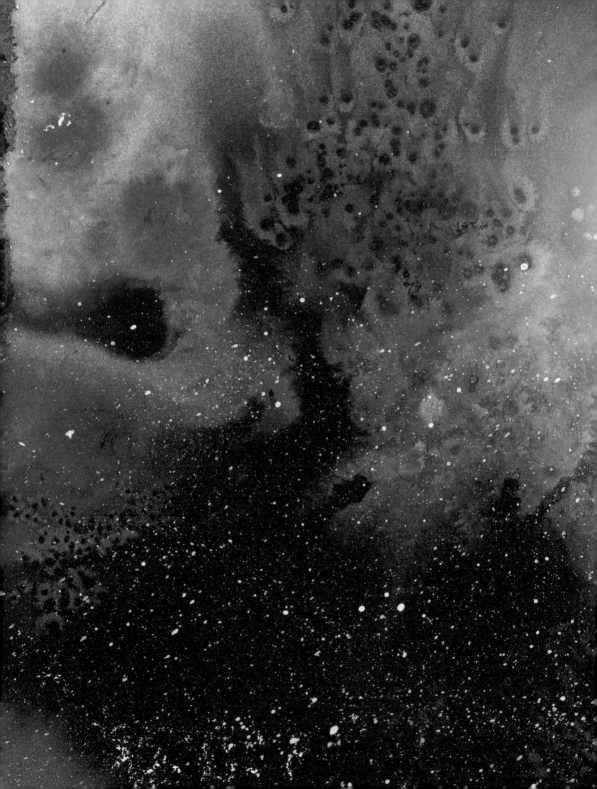

adventures after dusk

In this section, I invite you to go out and explore
the world of the night for yourself, with suggestions
for simple yet exciting adventures that will become
the start of your own magical night journey.

walking by twilight

We live in a noisy and distracting world, and often, the only time we can find a slice of peace is to take a walk after sundown, when everyone else has headed home for dinner or is cozying up in front of the television.

There is something very clarifying about a walk in the night, when the world around you melts away into the dark and you are left with the calming illusion of being alone with your thoughts. One of my favorite serenity walks is just a simple neighborhood walk along a quiet dirt path in a field wide open to the starry sky. A serenity walk is the yin to the wonder-walk's yang: rather than surrounding yourself with inspiration as a path to creativity, a serenity walk is quieter and calmer; it's about giving yourself a time to recenter and breathe. The world is full of wonder, but sometimes we need it to be full of peace, in order to nourish our soul and allow ourselves to recharge, ready for more creative adventures the next day.

take a serenity walk when you need to find quiet, stillness, and calm.

plan your serenity walk

Plan a week of daily twilight serenity walks. Each one can take just 15–30 minutes, after sunset, wherever it's quietest near your home, perhaps around the block, or a safe natural area—a beach or neighborhood park, for example. Observe how reconnecting to stillness and quiet feels. Record your experience here or in your night journal (see pages 16–17).

wonder-walking the night sky

Sometimes, instead of creating peace and calm, a twilight walk can bring excitement and awe. Walking beneath the night sky is most wondrous when it feels like our first encounter with it—delightful, enchanting, miraculous. Has familiarity dulled your experience? Try this activity:

✦ On a clear night, go outside on a walk, preferably somewhere wide open with low light pollution. If you cannot venture far, step out where you can see the night sky clearly—from a garden or a balcony works perfectly fine.

✦ Close your eyes and imagine yourself standing there at a time before your ancestors understood the science of the night sky. You might find yourself in a clearing in the middle of an ancient forest, or knee-deep in the shallows of a primeval sea. Clear your mind of all knowledge you might have of the stars, planets, and galaxies. Think of the sky abstractly, as if it's something mysterious and unknowable.

✦ With this lens on, walk the land around you as you practice observing different celestial phenomena with child-like curiosity—the moon, a shooting star, the patterns of "starlight" (constellations), and anything else that might be visible from where you are.

✦ Try spinning stories to interpret what you're seeing, just as the ancients did (see page 65). It will help make this exercise more visceral and memorable.

observations and interpretations of the
stars and night sky

_____

_____

_____

_____

_____

_____

_____

_____

_____

_____

feasting in the dark

When I was growing up in Southeast Asia, dining outdoors after sunset at night markets and open-air stalls were activities much looked forward to. There was a sense of leisure and festivity about the occasion: fairy lights strung in trees, great food, laughter and conversation, the cool evening air a much-welcomed reprieve from the tropical heat of the day. Since then, I've noticed that food always tastes better when partaken of outdoors, especially in the dimming hours after an evening hike, around a wilderness campfire, or at an everyday backyard barbecue.

There's something about dining in the dark that sharpens our tastebuds and heightens our appreciation for the food (and company) in front of us. It transforms an ordinary bottle of wine into delicious nectar, a simple rice dish cooked over a campfire into heavenly ambrosia, and an everyday meal into an enchanted culinary experience under an atmospheric canopy of stars.

This is why fancy restaurants dim the lights and set out glowing candles for memorable evening meals—it allows everything outside your table to melt away into darkness, with intimacy wrapping its arms around you and your companion(s). It says there is nothing more important right now than enjoying your meal and your company.

a midnight picnic

Plan a midnight picnic or nocturnal dining experience to explore whether food really does taste better outdoors at night. Try:

✦ A full-moon wonder-walk along the beach, followed by a slice of cake and ginger beer shared between friends or loved ones.

✦ Cooking dinner over a portable stove from the back of your car at a favorite nature spot.

✦ Hanging some fairy lights in your garden, setting a backyard table with a tablecloth and candles, and inviting friends over to dine outdoors with you.

Observe how it feels. How is it similar to or different from an intimate dinner out at a fancy restaurant? Is it better than dining indoors?

moon rituals

Moon rituals have taken place throughout history in various corners of the world as a way of celebrating and synchronizing with the cycle of life on Earth. All eight phases of the moon are celebrated, but the main times for ritual are the new moon, which is a time for new beginnings, and the full moon, which brings high energy to nurture our creative projects and allows us to flourish.

LABYRINTHS

The labyrinth is a deeply personal symbol to me—a reminder that life is a meandering journey that always brings us closer to our truths. Unlike a maze, there is only one route, and the entry point to the labyrinth is the same as the exit point. In the labyrinth, you walk to the center, which represents exploring the depth of your soul, before turning and following the path back out again. Labyrinths are part of many cultures, and have been used since ancient times to allow people to meditate and reflect as they journey on the physical path of the labyrinth and also on a spiritual path of discovery.

I'm fortunate to live five minutes away from a magical waterfront, and one of my favorite rituals is a moonlight labyrinth walk that never fails to leave me feeling utterly enchanted. The moon reflects off the surface of the nearby waters like diamonds scattered on grass, bathing the labyrinth's rock-lined path and the trees around me in an ethereal silvery glow like a scene straight from a magical tale.

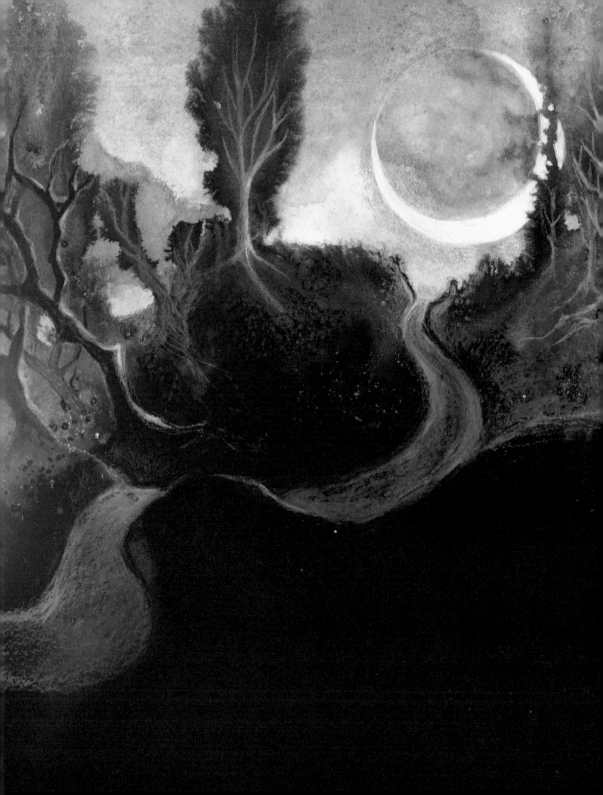

personal moonlight ritual

Plan your own moonlight ritual during a full moon to reconnect to lunar energy and the natural rhythms of life. It can take place somewhere outdoors that is special to you. Decide what you would like to focus on—accomplishing goals, or your sense of self—and build your ritual around that. For example, you might write a list of current projects and in your ritual search for answers on how to complete them, or create a meditation based on finding what allows you to be most authentic in your daily life.

If you are drawn to the labyrinth symbol, seek out one near you that you can walk in moonlight—the combination intensifies the experience.

Record your experience here or in your night journal (see pages 16–17).

_____

_____

_____

_____

_____

_____

starlight over dark waters

Three-quarters of our planet is underwater, and yet we know so little of what goes on in its darkest depths. We cannot see what happens even just beneath the surface of oceans, lakes, and large rivers when the sun sets. The dark sky reflected in the waters creates a vast inkiness that seems to stretch out infinitely, underscoring a black hole of human knowledge.

What happens at night out in the deep, watery dark? How can we reconnect to the most primordial of Earth's places? Being on the beach at night intensifies feelings of uncertainty and fear of the unknown—but what will you discover if you face your discomfort head-on?

take a nocturnal water adventure

Plan an overnight road trip to a large body of water nearby—it could be a lake, a large river, or the sea. If possible, camp or park nearby where you can safely walk along the shore or banks. Bring along a companion if needed.

Some nocturnal activities to explore on this adventure:

✦ If there are tide pools where you'll be going, take a UV torch for fluorescent treasure hunting.

✦ Observe the stars or moon reflected in the surface of the water. Think about past ocean navigators who traveled by learning the movement of the stars.

✦ Listen out for splashes in the waters. What do you think they might be? What other sounds can you hear?

✦ Watch the changing tides through the evening, and the next morning. Can you observe the relationship between the moon and the tides? Are there any nocturnal creatures hovering in the lapping waters? Why are they there?

✦ Record your feelings about the dark waters at night here or in your night journal (see pages 16–17). What did you learn about yourself or this place from your watery, nocturnal adventures?

your discoveries from your exploration of dark waters

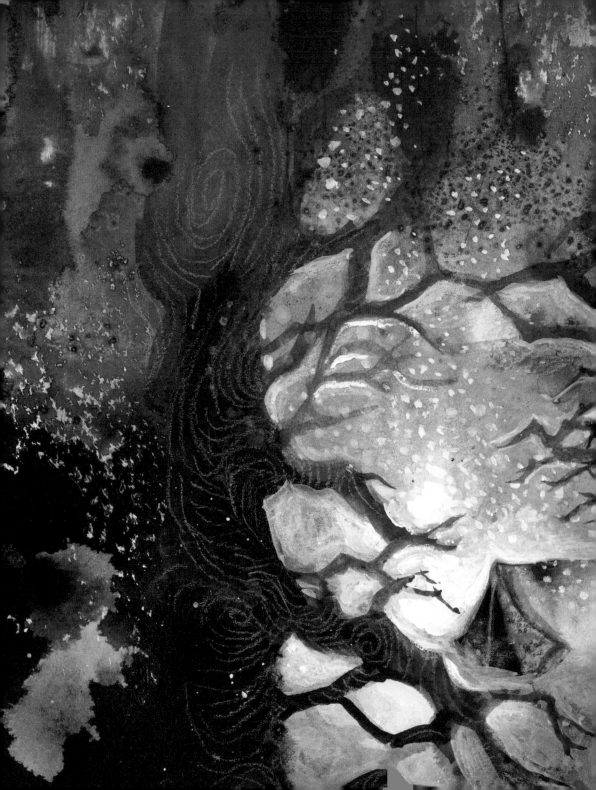

return to the hearth

Modern life has transformed the way we relate to the natural world, and we find ourselves gradually disconnected from it in a way that can be disruptive and even detrimental to our (and our planet's) well-being. Electricity allows us to work late into the night and ignore our circadian rhythms. We find ourselves overcommitted and overriding our natural rhythms and cycles, ultimately burning out because we forget that all living beings need consistent nourishment and replenishment. We are careless with Earth's precious resources because we feel apart from it in our cozy, artificially lit cocoons.

There is a reason why forest bathing and nature therapy are a thing. Being away from modern life and incessant phone notifications, emails, and responsibilities, and being with just the stars and the trees, can be enormously rejuvenating and healing. It reminds us of our aliveness, that we are connected to something bigger than ourselves. Nothing reinvigorates me faster than a camping trip when I am forced to turn off my phone.

camping under the stars

Plan a weekend camping trip. If you're new to camping, you might like to try a campground somewhere near home, or even stay in your backyard. If you're able to, try challenging yourself to primitive (wild) camping, where you have to walk to your chosen spot and there are no facilities. (In the UK, this type of camping is permitted only in parts of Scotland.) The goal is to experience what life would have been like before modern conveniences took over; to be alone with just the night sky, the ground under you, and the trees or ocean and animals.

As you lie on your sleeping bag under a canopy of stars, observe how it feels to return to a simpler life. What feels different about the night when you're far away from the city?

coming alive in the dark

Some of the most magnificent creatures in the animal kingdom are nocturnal. All around the world they have become surrounded by mythology and magic, because they are elusive and rarely seen in the light of day. The gray wolf, the red fox, the barn owl, the tiger, the coyote, the white rhino; just because we do not see them in broad daylight does not mean they aren't out there. Their world begins as ours retreats, after sunset, when we return to the sanctuary of our cozy, lit homes. Some, such as the deer and the rabbit, are crepuscular, coming alive in the eerie blue glow of twilight, and others, such as the wild boar and the mountain lion, are completely nocturnal—waiting until the cloak of darkness descends to hunt food, nest, or scout territories, leaving behind prints and scat as the only evidence of their ghostly presence. One year, it rained so hard where we lived that the trails around our home turned into mud and we found large paw prints of a mountain lion not five minutes from our front door. It was the closest we ever came to encountering this fierce and majestic creature in the wild.

do you know the invisible wild
that lives near you?

observing our nocturnal companions

Take some time to consider the world of nocturnal wildlife.

✦ Do you think that the mythology and magic surrounding animals such as the fox, the owl, or the wolf are a result of their nocturnal nature? Reread any local animal folklore and ponder this.

✦ Visit a local natural history center or refer to an app, such as iNaturalist, to learn about the nocturnal wildlife where you live. How does it change the way you think about these animals and their traits, habits, and significance to you?

✦ Are there any clues that there is a world rich with wildlife all around you after dark? Do you hear owl conversations at midnight? Are coyotes howling in the distance? Have you ever noticed wild boar tracks in any nearby forests or woodland?

IN SEARCH OF THE INVISIBLE WILD

Head out on a sunset wonder-walk in a nearby patch of wilderness and linger until it's completely dark. It's a great time to witness the invisible wild coming alive. Alternatively, take a walk on a moonless night. Bring a torch and, as always, refer to local guides on keeping you and the animals safe in the wild. While it is wonderful to be aware that such a glorious animal world exists after dark, we should be mindful and respectful of their needs on all our wonder-walks in nature. Humans have increasingly encroached on their natural habitats, and in many cases they are retreating further into the dark.

What can you hear and see? Where are you most likely to encounter signs of life? Keep your voices and other sounds low and ears pricked as you stroll in the dark. Record your experience here or in your night journal (see pages 16–17).

continuing your magical night journey

I hope that these pages have provided you with inspiration and a starting point to set off on your own adventure of wonder. Use the following pages to make a note of which activities have most developed your creativity and which ones you'd still like to explore further, or simply use the space to write freely.

what magic will you discover in the night?